UNLOCK YOUR POTENTIAL

UNLOCK YOUR POTENTIAL

Achieving Peak Performance

B. VINCENT

QuantumQuill Press

CONTENTS

CHAPTER 1

Introduction

Your morals, ethics, and integrity will become your unwavering duty, enabling you to see everything through with vision and clarity. These dynamics, when correctly adjusted and guided will help you to unleash your inner passion. They will cast fear aside, and in alignment with knowledge will unlock endless possibilities. Ways will open, and like the peacock who spreads its wings, they will dance through life, guaranteeing that light and laughter encompasses all they touch. The dynamics in the framework will guide you, uphold self-respect and self-belief, and show by example. In the right conjunction, they will ensure that goodness abounds, and make you every bit a Phenomena. They will make you realize treat triumph as the guaranteed reward of every dream.

This book explores the key principles essential for achieving peak performance, no matter how high the challenges. The key principles are as follows: eight indispensable dynamics which, when worked on, will enable you to unlock boundless potential – the VIP formula. Create the right framework, or foundation, which supports all peak performance dynamics. The correct framework will enable you to hold your value systems in place. These same values will pull you back into place, ready to plough forward. They incline your inner soul toward the tenacity, wisdom, courage, and vision to persevere through the storms, and underpin everything they do.

1.1. Definition of Peak Performance

We must recognize that people consist of their overall personality. People living at home, amongst family and friends, at work, and in society are the same person. Most of us separate our family behavior from business behavior. The logic, however, is that if people are achievers at home, they must be able to transfer these skills to the business arena. The question, then, is why don't they? What is the difference between my home hurdle and business hurdle where I seem to get stuck and not achieve more? Achievers say these hurdles don't exist. This statement differentiates achievers from others. From achievers' perspective, there is no difference between people who get stuck and those who achieve.

The first two questions to consider are: What is peak performance? Who is a high performer or a peak performer? We all use the term "peak performance" or "high performer" or "peak performer" very freely. It comes in various contexts in business, sports, tennis, baseball, etc. What do we mean? How is peak performance viewed, defined, or described? Peak performance is a result – it is about achieving tangible results consistently over time despite changes in the environment. I call that the high-performance promise.

CHAPTER 2

Setting Goals

When you start setting your goals, the first part of the process is to define what you want and what it is most important to you. This is the basic criteria of practical goal setting. You have to start by being super clear about what you want in every aspect of your life, from your relations, through money and psychological, spiritual development factors to your health and leisure, all this to seven key areas of your life. Goals must respect a set of basic criteria, as well as some extra criteria. But the important thing is always to pay attention to how the actual purpose you are setting will make you feel when you have achieved it. You must always consider first what makes you happy, what excites you, what makes you ecstatic, not what makes you feel frustrated and unhappy when you feel incomplete. When you feel your purpose and how happy you will be if you will achieve it, then it is the right purpose for you. When you're defining your goals, you should complete the related fields. No incomplete or ambiguous sentences, everything must be as clear, specific, realistic and seen in the positive sense as possible.

Setting and going after goals is one of the main elements of success. Every goal is an objective. The more ambitious your goals are, the stronger you will be required to develop. Nevertheless, your goals should be practical as well as them to be achieved in a reasonable period of time, and the efforts taken to achieve them should not be overwhelming, must not be more difficult than the actual effort and amount of knowledge required to achieve them. Setting goals is a very powerful process for thinking about your ideal future and for motivating you to achieve your dreams, it can help you turn your vision into reality. The objective setting strategy can also help you organize your thoughts and, even more, help you see and make your way to the realization of your vision and turn that vision into reality.

2.1. SMART Goals

This is believed to be the step in smart development goals that shows form and structure. In this, a goal needs to be clearly defined that says what it is that I want to achieve, how my development plan is going to progress, and what is required to know when the goal is achieved. Evidence of the skills, mindset, values that are going to be displayed should be clearly defined. The people that are going to work with me to achieve the goal have to be identified. From experience over the years, when dealing with clients, the start off with what is it that you want has to be clearly defined. A lot of people struggle with giving a clear answer to the question. This is the first step and it needs to have a clear focus and a clear picture of what success will look like. A starting point that can assist you is to look at your goal and find a close synonym or another way to describe it.

Secondly, when going smart, the goal has to be measurable, to identify indicators for success or failure. It is the cornerstone of the smart objective. What can you measure that will help find that you are on the right path, that indicates that you have a mind development plan? There are no half measures when it comes to measuring a goal, it is either measurable or it is not.

In the first phase of smart goals, there has to be a clear understanding of what the purpose is, putting some detail around what happened. Why it is that and then clearly understanding what I want to achieve there. This step is the most important, as knowing clearly what you want will help create a level of clarity of why you need to do it and how you are going to go about it. Because when there is a clearly defined idea around what you want, the universe has no choice but to help. The universal law states that.

2.2. Long-term vs Short-term Goals

If Basha had only hiked in her local area within a fifty-mile radius of her town, her long-term goals of hiking the Sierras, the Appalachian and Rocky Mountains would never come to be. By climbing numerous smaller mountains, she was able to really understand her abilities and increase them. Also, most people do not have the time or ability to temporarily abandon their everyday lives to engage in long-term goals. Many people have families or jobs or other duties which require them to stay in one place, and even though they may forever dream of climbing Mount Rainier, for instance, the best they can hope to achieve at that specific moment in time is climbing a smaller peak or going on a long hike.

Are your goals long-term or short-term? That's an important question to consider. Long-term goals have an established end, and their purpose is to help give direction and focus to your life. In contrast, short-term goals are stepping stones that can help you move closer to your ultimate long-term goals. Although short- and long-term goals may seem dissimilar, they actually work hand-in-hand. Short-term goals lay the stable groundwork for your long-term aims.

CHAPTER 3

Time Management

Unfortunately, individuals see time management issues as a problem for their organizations. An individual, personal problem is often seen as something that needs to be resolved after solving a larger and more complex external problem. They see the problem of time as an obvious matter of a person trying to do too many tasks during working hours. On the surface, the prevention of peak productivity seems to be the result of incorrect time management. Then Brady's whole life leadership course on time management, time management results from ignorance and neglect. Some employees view such problems as either subject to class or status specialization, often as a factor sponsored by a lack of title responsibility, supervision or respect for the organization.

Time management is the most basic self-management skill. It is an essential responsibility to realize peak performance. The work settings, technological changes, and global market conditions all demand time management. The development stages of time management are known as past or traditional productivity management, charting and task focus, and activity focus. Self-management is the process of looking at a person, self, to understand the abilities, responsibilities, and ways of living of a new or layered person. It makes individuals aware of themselves, and aware of the things they like and worry about. When you can control your thoughts, emotions, your company and nature, you can manage your energy and day and increase your productivity.

3.1. Prioritizing Tasks

Say for an instance that Martin has a long list of tasks to handle today. He knows what he wants and every inch of him wants to vanquish every written task at once. But can he do it perfectly on time? Some would say yes while most people who are pessimists and rational individuals would say "absolutely not". Why not challenge the latter response? With the right understanding and mastery of the science behind the prioritization of tasks, beating deadlines and destroying your competition can be a walk in the park. With proper planning, a person can acquire greater focus and higher productivity than a self-driven worker. By planning one's days ahead, the top-level manager obtains a more flexible base for better prioritization, establishing a workplace that can focus on executing hard and important tasks within a shorter time frame.

Every person—successful or not—has 24 hours each day. But why are others excelling more than we do? The main reasons might be the lack of sense of urgency and inability to prioritize their activities. By ranking our tasks according to their urgency and importance, we attain a higher level of focus, thus accomplishing more important things earlier in the day. People who do this greatly lessen the busy work they encounter later in the day. Once one succeeds in finding the root of daily complexities, everything will flow smoothly, leading to their desired results. Our mind is continuously processing various information every our awake moments, trying to handle various conflicting interests and reshape our plans and actions to suit the issues especially today.

3.2. Creating a Schedule

One of the first things you will want to do is to create a schedule. We talked earlier about the importance of scheduling, and we'll go into more detail in the next chapter. I am a firm believer in working smart, and a large part of that is making time for both your physical and emotional well-being as well as professional development. The other part is focus, being able to concentrate on the task at hand, whatever task that might be. The schedule we will talk about won't be complicated and it's really something you can make use of regardless of your position in the organization. The heart of it is to be very thoughtful with what your time gets spent on.

What this schedule looks like will ultimately depend on your personal routine, and what you choose to use it for. However, I recommend scheduling a few regularly occurring events every week. These might include time at the gym, quiet time to read up on some research you're interested in, time spent practicing a speech, or a rehearsal for an upcoming webinar or presentation.

One of the first things you will want to do is to create a schedule. I am a firm believer in working smart, and a large part of that is making time for both your physical and emotional well-being as well as professional development. The other part is focus, being able to concentrate on the task at hand, whatever task that might be. The schedule we will talk about won't be complicated and it's really something you can make use of regardless of your position in the organization. The heart of it is to be very thoughtful with what your time gets spent on.

CHAPTER 4

Mindset

Author Natalie Rothstein provides a great start for the chapter on How to Achieve Instant Focus and Concentration. She asserts that "the right mindset is absolutely critical." She describes how to foster a mindset that doesn't contradict the brain's natural tendencies to "daydream and lose focus," but harnesses them and even reward the brain's naturally creative processes "before you even begin to work." Her ideas on how to achieve the "right mindset" include visualization exercises, reminders, the right amount of time, setting an agenda, bedtime tasking, and physical movement. These habits will help you lay a foundation for an effective mindset. One way to help switch from "unproductive mental daydreaming" to mental alertness, Rothstein suggests rebounding between daydreaming and focusing, rather than trying to make our natural mental state of focus, with all its limitations, fit some sort of idealized perfect mental state. Author LaRae Quy also delves into the importance of mindset.

Elton Alderman's chapter, What is a Mindset? provides a clear definition of mindset, describes its essential characteristics, and differentiates between the two most fundamental types of mindsets, "those for growth and those for fixed." As a coach or individual, it is helpful to understand the implications of each type of mindset and how to foster or change these mindsets, or to manage and channel the results of having each type of mindset in a productive manner.

4.1. Growth Mindset vs Fixed Mindset

The growth mindset is something that makes complete sense, but the hang-up is how to put the concept into practice. Dweck suggests that one of the most significant solutions to putting the growth mindset into practice is to recognize that what a person picks to practice may not give the desired results in the short term or even possibly the long term. Effort, challenge, and persistence are some of the best strategies to achieve learning and growth. Parents, teachers, and coaches know how much effort is needed to learn, improve, correct failure, and a willingness to make mistakes. To reach the potential that one is striving for, make the necessary efforts and undertake the unavoidable challenges. Mistakes are the next opportunity that one should seek to obtain the intelligence, knowledge, and skills that one craves. A growth mindset provides for the translation of a love of learning and a free will to invest in long-term self-improvement.

The concept of the growth mindset, coined by Carol Dweck, is significant. She has studied the area for many years. Her key point is that people who believe they can grow are more likely to succeed and those who don't believe they can grow are more likely to fail. The differences in success and failures of these beliefs are prolific and readily apparent in humans. The concept is simple: a growth mindset is where one believes they can develop their mind, talents, and abilities beyond what they currently are. In contrast, someone with a fixed mindset believes that their intelligence, talents, and abilities are fixed and cannot be changed. These beliefs are deeply ingrained and contribute to a person's behaviors and ultimately the individual's moral and ethical choices. The foundation of the growth mindset exists throughout many cultures and is a universally accepted concept. A growth mindset within a person determines their views about themselves, their willingness to take risks and to embrace new challenges, and their ability to recognize and change their flaws. A person with a growth mindset is much more likely to welcome feedback from others.

4.2. Overcoming Limiting Beliefs

It is this emotion which makes the child believe that any goal they set for themselves will be reached. But then we grow up and forget how this worked. As adults, we started to elect limitations for ourselves, creating limits for our goals. We are able to construct much stronger walls for our beliefs and live by what is possible or not possible in everyday life. Our wishes and dreams are converted into achievable goals. The decision-making process of what can be achieved or not is influenced by our beliefs. We handed this power over to our beliefs and we are not even aware of this fact. It is up to us to believe, consciously, in what we intend to achieve in life. You need to believe in the extraordinary potential that you possess in order to achieve great results.

According to Anthony Robbins, a limiting belief is nothing more than a belief that a person has which limits his or her potential. Putting this in another way, it is a guideline set in your mind that dictates some form of limitation on you. Robbins finishes by stating that the limitation a person realizes is his or her own; in fact, they limit themselves. It is common to find children who roundly claim that they want to become astronauts, princesses, mountaineers or anything else they can think of. No goal is too big for them to wish to achieve. They set their goals based on events that they focus on, situations involving or even toys, stories and fantasies. In general, they choose extreme situations or characters and end up with a belief that such characters always win or the situations always have a good ending. A child's belief is very strong and it involves a lot of emotion.

"No one should think ever again of the great potential to achieve any new goal, whether for financial success or any other kind of success. Such joy will be felt upon achieving any goal that has been set no limit. The important secret of good results is what steps the logical to understand someone in great potential." - John Markovski

CHAPTER 5

Motivation

Micro-waves move massive objects. The answer lies in micro-behaviors that: Every individual, whether he/and positive: Do I attend every meeting and follow through with exercises keeping discussion intense and? Or do I stare at a screen and online as it keeps be? Do I make waves before my appraiser or boss? Do I avoid attending team events and use my time? Did I shut eyes and mind? Do I avoid eye contact and hope others do the same? Do I mostly create and solve the problems away from the glare of the keyboard and screen? Do I sulk at someone's success or do I take part in the celebrations, tiny waves simulations. Building micro-behaviors are faith only on the screen; of the urgency even if it means continuous weeks having values; values solely influence motivation: petty jobs.

Microbehaviors move you to what? Micro waves over eon's impact what? Winning the small battles impart into the larger battles which will bear fruit. In 2013 Microsoft Deep Thought supercomputer pronounced at Pro Chess "Move 37 is wrong". Kasparov realizes; it was correct. Confounds by it, he was unable to rezoned it because Kasparov is at the threshold of peak not the role of a mentor. Proved by computer. Lesions like micro behavior, into whomever live and work, help you flower into freedoms and become a beacon to others to build a wall of microbehaviors: the sum total of micro-behaviors win battles nod there are no language or cultural barriers because of their simplicity, they make you a peak performer. They give you mental, moral, and material satisfaction. They decide to sweep or move on. They decide to have humility or arrogance. They decide to have common sense or take foolish risks. They give you inner and outer joy. Rewards of display out of grandeur of glow.

5.1. Intrinsic vs Extrinsic Motivation

Intrinsic motivation comes from the inside and arises from the individual interest to learn and practice in order to succeed. It has been determined as a strong personal characteristic, which is essential for one's happiness, life satisfaction and positive experience. The other type of motivation is extrinsic, arising when people act with certain motivation, to gain particular outcomes which are separate from activities themselves. People perform an action because they are pressured, punished or tempted by rewards and benefits purpose. Many of the employees get their training not for what they can win after them, but because the program will bring them some professional advancement or pay raise. Furthermore, extrinsic motivation links to receiving a high promotion by getting high grades, rather than learning, master new knowledge or develop a relationship with the teacher.

For people to grow they need deeper motivation. Deeper motivation means being more self-motivated, being driven by motives which go beyond simple self-interest. Being truly driven involves doing things because they are important in their own right. This is often referred to as intrinsic motivation. There are few things which are genuinely indispensable and to find them people need to become deeply engaged in doing what they really love to do. Such activities are a powerful predictor of positivity in life.

CHAPTER 6

Focus

Thinking about the things that you do well is a huge motivator. If you focus on the things that you do well, you can utilize and improve these strengths. Talk to yourself, in a positive way. When you tell yourself you can succeed, you are more likely to succeed. This is especially important for athletes. For most people, consistently hitting bogeys on your golf performance, low points in your tennis matches, or the like is not helpful. Stop thinking about your faults; attention to them just illustrates what you need to change them. Instead, stay focused on your strengths and abilities. Remember how well you hit the serve in your last match, or the wonderful putt you achieved during a golfing game. Keep the pressure off and the outcome will be positive.

The sixth skill that you'll need to train your brain to develop is your ability to focus. Many people don't develop this skill, simply because they give attention to anything that comes their way. They listen to others' conversations even when they are not directed at them, they react in their minds to email notifications and with smartphones have 24/7 access to the internet. Time management research has shown that people waste a lot of time on digital overload. To prevent all this from happening, put a block on some activities and focus completely on the task at hand for a while. Your lifespan may depend on it.

6.1. Eliminating Distractions

Effort and productivity aren't the same. How many of us brag about our work through catchy pet phrases – such as "working hard"? You may revel in your efforts, but you're wasting your time if that effort isn't paired with achievement. Be sure to give yourself breathing room to achieve productivity. Aim for less—a trait common to elite producers. Reach new capacities instead of old habits. Embrace the spirit of less-is-more today, and boost your growth. If leaving your phone unattended tips your anxiety scales, set times throughout the day when you put the phone away and dive into a task – aim for a blend of 20 minutes of focused work followed by a 10-minute phone check. Experiment with time intervals to track your anxiety levels. Explore practices to help build self-discipline over time, including scheduling tasks across a finite time frame. As you grow comfortable with increased periods of deep work, track your improved work performance to inspire continued growth. Value quality over quantity. Find small ways to unplug from the digital world, and increase your ties to real, human experiences.

Distraction is one of the greatest threats to attaining high performance at any level. Beyond the noise and visual triggers linked to your immediate environment, you have personal distractions/weaknesses, technological distractions, and those from people in your inner and outer circle of relationships. Being distracted pokes holes in your mental, cognitive, and output abilities. They interfere with your thinking, feeling, and ultimate behavior. Addressing your distractions will not only let you achieve work progression in your personal settings and in your external work assignments, but give you mastery over legitimate job deliverables associated with your work.

6.2. Deep Work Techniques

Sleep and exercise are important on their own; however, they also impact deep work techniques, while recovery and rest are necessary to ensure deep work and flow dynamics. Striving for an ideal work-life balance, best supported by a routine that starts slowly, gears up gradually and winds down, should keep everyone motivated. Deep work is demanding, requires a priori decision of time allocation and full conscious presence; moreover, the deliberate balance of deep and shallow work embedded in one's daily routine helps build the necessary skills. Procrastination is an adaptation and harmonizes the healthy evolution towards living a diverse, rich and complex life with dilemmas of the sort "should I practice the violin or go kayaking?" Similarly, decision fatigue can wear people down and drain their self-regulatory, leading to poor choices and procrastination. The concept of deep work succumbs to the same problem, with the use of energy and concentration as finite resources that can get depleted. Efforts require self-regulation, reducing the individual's abilities for more complex tasks; therefore, by the end of the day, energy and self-regulatory resources are depleted and the motivation to write a grant dwindles. Building routines instead of relying exclusively on willpower will help with this issue, as schedules can structure daily work and commit specific time slots to deep work.

One can build a deep work practice by focusing first on one hour of uninterrupted work, increasing gradually to two to four hours without interruptions, while intensively concentrating and blocking distractions. Spending the day deliberately switching between deep and shallow work phases will help to maintain a sustainable balance, which builds resilience and ability to achieve peak performance when needed. Ultimately, the goal is to build a portfolio of deep and shallow work activities, based on foundational goals and routines, such as the one depicted in Fig. 13. The deep work parts should be hedged with routines for rest and recovery, to ensure intensity and a strong focus. Over time, you should increase the portfolio with more meaningful, personally rewarding, high-value work; while time should also be allocated for community and fun, it is important not to overindulge in entertainment or be a "cry for help" responder, as they provide only trivial joy and are negatively associated with extended levels of unproductive internet usage.

CHAPTER 7

Resilience

Have you ever listened to the nonstop woes of a friend and found yourself thinking, "Seriously?" Resilient people have that reaction. I challenge you to treat your endurance as far more precious than many have. Reserve your emotional social comfort zone for those you hold dear, and the causes and crises that truly register with you; use laughter, constructive criticism, and other methods to help those resilient people see that they, too, have the strength to rise. One of the more pervading myths developing over the years resulting in a codependence epidemic is tied to self-care. Despite the popular culture emphasis, more than baby boomers actually just awoke in police custody to this word and made a run for the border. Whether the professional or personal self-mission is to help all, this pervasive view honors service over self-worth. Protect your well-being; exercise, sleep, and joyful hobbies are armor. Release the mantra "I am the only one who can help." Ask yourself the question resilience has pondered: "What inspired a desire to intervene?" and other activities could likely end the saga as quickly. Input energy into practical, thematic responses and help the community gain strength or seek professional support. Remember, the wellspring of strength may be discovered as your mission shifts. Be sure that helping others does not compromise your pause.

Resilience is popular these days, cropping up in myriad discussions around change or in criticism of the past generation for being protective helicopter parents. However, many of us face situations every day that require emotional stamina, and the faculty of resilience seems in shorter supply with each generation. In this section, we will explore what resilience really means, its value in performance, and how your attitudes and behaviors are a big step in fueling it. We will conclude with conducting an assessment and a few building strategies.

7.1. Dealing with Setbacks

9. Finally, charter is subscribe to the philosophy of "you learn from every defeat." So, as soon as you start to feel better, take the time to reflect on events that occurred and think about how you can use these insights to move onward and upwards.

8. Celebrate past achievements, big or small, that come to mind; this will help augment self-worth.

7. Expose yourself to situations where you minimized your reactions to setbacks or where you have adopted a "mindful" approach of non-reaction or acceptance toward others. Reflect on these events and how you can replicate your non-reaction to setbacks.

6. Recall past setbacks in your life and remember how you overcame these obstacles through time and reflection.

5. Remind yourself that you can still achieve your long-term goals and that there are alternative paths to reach these.

4. Reframe the setback so that it is seen as temporary or specific to a certain situation (instead of generalizing the fault to a person's character or overall performance).

3. Accept the emotion you are feeling, label it, and accept that it's a part of being human. We all face setbacks at some point in time.

2. Switch from immediate action to patience and reflection. Push the pause button on your angry or fearful response, and count to ten. Take three deep breaths (inhalations and exhalations for a count of three). This will help reduce the initial emotional intensity.

1. Recognize your emotions when faced with a setback. Regardless of whether it is a feeling of anger, fear, anxiety or sorrow, allow yourself to feel these genuine emotions without judgment.

We have all experienced setbacks – failed exams, missed promotions, a shocker of a presentation. Here's ten ways to regain your composure and get back on the bandwagon.

CHAPTER 8

Self-care

Whatever demands you face, in the workplace or in your personal life, it's always best to be in the best shape you can be. This doesn't mean denying yourself of treats or pleasures, but being disciplined to make sure you're effective as and when you need to be. Be a role model on those demanding days when we are all tempted to reach for chocolate, alcohol or recreational drugs—resist the temptation and you will be an example for everyone else having a tough day. In turn, you will feel more proud of yourself the next day. Feeling healthy, strong, and purposeful attracts a positive mental approach. When you burn out and have done everything you can, it's the colleagues and friends and family who remind you to take time out to look after yourself who are your biggest allies.

What is self-care, and how can it improve your personal effectiveness at work and in other areas of your life? The concept is simple – taking time out to look after yourself to ensure you're in the best physical, emotional, and mental condition possible. The actions it covers may not always sound like fun—sleeping for 7 or 8 hours a night, eating healthily, doing regular exercise, and other activities that help your long-term health. If you don't look after yourself in the short term, you're more likely to suffer physical, emotional, or mental health problems which could take you away from work. That's why self-care is so important.

8.1. Importance of Rest and Recovery

Recovery is a very complex and unique concept because not one size fits everyone. In fact, how we recover is as unique as our fingerprints. Stretching, fuel, sleep, decompression and relaxation are all important elements necessary post-rehab, post-exercise, and post-work. After a session, the body needs rest, stretch, and refueling to move through the process of repairing muscle tissue. Each different routine will require a different combination of these essential elements. You need to have enough time to recharge your batteries. Many people overlook their resting nutrition or they often eat too soon or delay their nutrients or other elements they require to help in the necessary repair of those aching muscles and recharge the batteries. Our body has an amazing and complex ability to restore, recovery and repair itself. This is deeply needed in must get back in balance.

Rest and recovery is crucial. Overtraining and overworking can reduce the effectiveness of your workouts, increase your risk of injury, and can decrease your performance. Recovery between exercise repetitions or sets is vital to maintain the quality of session and to help to avoid injury. Recovery from intense exercise is as important as the training session itself. All gains are made when we rest, and that's the solid truth. Remember that you are not what you lift, you are your ability to recover from what you lift. When we do not allow ourselves proper recovery time, and this can affect our mental as well as our physical health. We are unique in our capacity to do many things each day, but eventually all of us need the time to recover. Our rest requirements depend on who we are, what we are doing, our fitness level, and the energy we use in our daily activity and performances.

8.2. Nutrition and Exercise

Physical exercise and working out are as important as good nutrition when it comes to achieving peak performance. Because physical exercise has so many positive effects on the body, it also makes for a healthier body and brain. Working out not only helps reduce tension and stress, but also makes for a better mood: after 10 minutes, we usually feel better! Furthermore, performing musculoskeletal exercises can actually help increase your discipline and powers of concentration. When you're working out, you increase your blood flow which means more oxygen rich blood to your brain. These effects could make for healthier and better functioning neurons. Participating in sports and exercising is also a great way to make new friends and build on your social network.

Food is your fuel. That's why some foods are better than others if you want to unlock your own potential and achieve peak performance. During studying, your brain actually uses up 20% of your total energy and 25% of the oxygen in your body. Your body normally uses 20% of your energy and 15% of your oxygen. Not only does your brain demand more energy and oxygen while working hard, it also produces large amounts of waste products that have to be removed so you can work effectively. Eating too much or the wrong kind of food can even increase the production of these waste products. If that happens, you get tired and you feel less fit. Also, your powers of concentration might dwindle. Stress obviously does the same thing and affects our brain's functioning. However, you'll get the best results from yourself if you feed your body and brain the right way.

CHAPTER 9

Mindfulness

The practice of mindfulness largely involves refining attention. Meditation practice trains the mind and can develop improved primary attention to work-related tasks. Given the endless distractions in modern work environments, the ability to regulate attention is paramount. Typically, our minds never cease engaging with thought processes, which distract us from the present. The more evolved and advanced your meditation practice becomes, the better equipped you are to pay attention to all activities that involve and reflect your capacity to perceive, think, and incorporate all the acknowledged and constant reflection, thereby achieving mindfulness relational play. Techniques to set focus renewal or re-regulation are also useful, particularly since good leaders have the ability to direct attention to achieve desired goals. Mindful people are better equipped memory and emotional regulation and learn that mindfulness is beneficial through practice, experience, and feedback. Mindful awareness users are rare and do not exist because living in a state of mindfulness is neither natural nor part of human development. In fact, most individuals are not mindful minute to minute because the inherent capacity to reflect on feelings and information details is limited by goal-oriented awareness.

Complete attention to the present moment. This definition is simple, but not easy for most people to put into practice. One of the hallmarks of mindfulness is the ability to focus attention with minimal distraction; this practice has been shown to increase feelings of hope and curiosity about what forces in the world shape our lives. Regular mindfulness practice contributes to mastery, the ability to influence the global outcome for one's goals through intention, planning, and cognitive mastery. A state of mindfulness promotes a general mood of happiness and has been associated with positive emotions, increase positive attitude, and good physical well-being. There is abundant evidence and growing acceptance of the value of mindfulness practice. One of the greatest benefits is improved focus or concentration. The ability to concentrate within the conscious human experience is at the core of ultimate performance. Great work and peak performance all require deep thought and focus. Mindfulness is a moist and culture and lifestyle.

9.1. Practicing Mindfulness Techniques

Mindfulness is the intentional, accepting, non-judgmental focus in the present moment of thoughts and emotions originating from the Buddhist religion. The practice of learning to be in the present moment leads to increased effectiveness in the execution of performance tasks. When individuals are in the present moment, their attention moves away from the past and future, protecting their working memory from being disrupted, leading to lower confusion anxiety, and finally, optimal levels of sports performance. Due to its capacity to stretch athletic discipline, the Asian practice of mindfulness is gaining increasing attention from the West over the past years. Identifying the role it plays in sport and its possible functions.

Exercise is a well-known coping technique when stress is high. In a study conducted at the University of Texas at Austin, 171 students performed a challenging task of making their way through an emotional speech. They were afterward instructed to perform one of three activities: sitting quietly (control group), exercising on treadmills, or practicing mindfulness (a yoga-based practice) and meditation. Thirty minutes later, students in all three groups again recorded their anxiety level and took a memory test. The students in the mindfulness group showed the next corresponding levels of working memory capacity and confusion. Whereas students in the exercise group and the control group scored significantly higher levels than on some both working memory capacity and some confusion because participants in the mindfulness treatment condition demonstrated less confusion and better working memory, results imply that mindfulness may be a better technique in reducing the cognitive deficits that have been linked to test anxiety. Subsequent studies show that mindfulness is not limited to yoga only but can be generalized to other types of relaxation techniques.

CHAPTER 10

Continuous Learning

To remain competitive in the business world and a master in your field, you should read, study, re-evaluate techniques and apply new findings to your job while assessing their effectiveness. This will add an entirely new dimension to your coaching and create a personal, fresh, unique approach that makes everyone quickly want to listen and learn from you and have fun. Keep on learning and growing your skills, knowledge and capabilities as a coach. Use continuous learning daily to help you get your skills to a point where you could be considered a 'professional' coach. Never becoming complacent with where you are at, you are always looking to learn more and keep up-to-date with new studies and professional developments. It takes time to evolve and get to the next level in your profession and as a coach. To be seen as an expert, you must know your subject matter inside out and understand how it fits into the wider and ever-evolving picture. Refine your coaching skills and ensure that you continuously grow as a business person. If you stop learning, you become less valuable. You have to evolve. As your career develops and time becomes one of the scarcest resources available, it's important to fold continuous learning activities into your life. Ongoing learning is more than just increasing our smarts; it is about knowing where we struggle, identifying a solution, and committing to our struggle.

There is no such thing as an expert. No matter how much you know about your chosen field, there is always more to learn. The day you think you've heard it all is the day you've left yourself open to someone else's competitive edge. Continuous learning is more than a way to stay informed or to build new skills. It is a state of mind that constantly looks for ways to make you and/or your company better. It's crucial to your performance potential. Why do actors, athletes, adults, artists, authors, children, leaders, employees, students do what they do? They do it for the rush. The rush that comes when they've just done something that they didn't think they could do. Everyone does things that help them get better, physically, mentally, spiritually, etc. Don't wait too long to take another risk. Bateson's Sequence on the perception-action cycle shows that everything we do or experience (except for reflexes) consists of this simple but flexible loop of perception and action. Every act we perform is based on an assessment of results of previous similar acts and there-fore everybody is learning. The flexibility comes into play because we have the ability to compare results to our expectations, decide if further action is warranted and to modify our behavior as needed. It is the need to continually revise our perceptions that allows us to learn from novel or unexpected events with an improvement that on a statistical basis leads to a better performance of the ADLs (activities of daily living).

10.1. Personal Development Strategies

So often people make the mistake of pursuing money or power or some piece of 'happiness' in their lives rather than pursuing the self-improvement of themselves that would inevitably lead them to their desired results. Imagine a person that becomes filthy rich. Does this person suddenly transform into someone who likes or dislikes a differ-ent kind of food? Do people start liking or disliking them based on their wealth? People are no different. Our greatest strengths and our most stubborn strengths come from people's 'custom habits'.

Ten years from now who you become will depend on the books you read and the company you keep. It does not matter how much you know about personal development and peak performance strategies –

it is what you do with that knowledge that truly counts. Wanting to become more successful is not enough. To achieve anything you must first be convinced to change or modify a particular custom, habit or way of interacting with others. The success of any of these options is then influenced by your ability to adopt new behaviours, understand and adhere to new and effective ways of communication, reach common goals and implement positive results.

* Introduction * Why Personal Development? * Personal Development Strategies * S.M.A.R.T Goals * The Power of Positive Declarative Statements * Affirmation * Visualisation * Mental Rehearsals and Inner Seeing * Ways to Increase Your Confidence * Final Words

Topics discussed in the lecture included the history of the subject, key concepts, real-world applications, and future trends in research. The guest speaker shared personal experiences and insights, sparking engaging discussions among the audience. Overall, the lecture was informative and thought-provoking, leaving attendees with a deeper understanding of the topic.